English
Activity Book

for ages 5-6

This CGP book is bursting with fun activities to build up children's skills and confidence.

It's ideal for extra practice to reinforce what they're learning in primary school. Enjoy!

Published by CGP

Editors:
Rachel Craig-McFeely, Catherine Heygate, Harry Millican, Katya Parkes,
Rebecca Russell

With thanks to Robbie Driscoll and Alison Griffin for the proofreading.

With thanks to Jan Greenway for the copyright research.

ISBN: 978 1 78908 531 0

Printed by Elanders Ltd, Newcastle upon Tyne.
Cover and graphics used throughout the book © www.edu-clips.com
Cover design concept by emc design ltd.

Text, design, layout and original illustrations © Coordination Group Publications Ltd. (CGP) 2020
All rights reserved.

Photocopying this book is not permitted, even if you have a CLA licence.
Extra copies are available from CGP with next day delivery • 0800 1712 712 • www.cgpbooks.co.uk

Contents

Nouns

How It Works

Nouns are words that name things. These words are all nouns:

hat chair sunshine sunglasses

Now Try These

1. Write the correct noun from the box next to each picture.

shorts

spade bucket

shell

 ....

 ....

2. Circle the words that are nouns.

book   lemon   hard

later   quickly   horse

shoe   car   nice

3. Circle the noun in each sentence.

He went on the slide.

I have a purple coat.

She made a tasty cake.

Your cat is hungry.

The water was very cold.

4. Complete each sentence with a noun from the box above it.

tiny	sand	later	slowly

I played in the ....

swimming	old	splashed	hamster

My sister has a pet ....

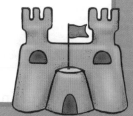

How many different nouns can you spot in the picture?

Can you write them down?

How did it go? Do you know your nouns? Tick a box.

Verbs

Verbs are doing or being words.

 The girl waves.

 She plays.

 The boy catches.

The verb needs to match the person doing the action.

He kicks.

 They kick.

Now Try These

1. Colour in the prizes that have verbs on them.

4

2. Circle the sentences that use the right verb.

Ivy are the winner.

I have brown hair.

We read our books.

You bake a cake.

Lexi and Ben goes to school.

3. Fill in the gap in each sentence with the right verb.

| swim | swims |

Noah .... really fast.

| ride | rides |

They .... their bikes.

| do | does |

I .... the splits.

An Extra Challenge

Class 1C always get warmed up before P.E. Can you describe what each child does? Use the verbs in the box to help you. How would the verbs change if you were doing the actions?

Example:
Ed jumps.
I jump.

~~jump~~

stretch

run

skip

Did you race through these pages? Give a box a tick.

Making sentences

A sentence is a group of words. The words need to be in the right order for a sentence to make sense.

Simon

 Simon bow pink wears a.

This sentence does not make sense.
The words are in the wrong order.

 Simon wears a pink bow.

This sentence does make sense.
The words are in the right order.

Now Try These

1. Draw lines to join the parts of the sentences so they make sense.

It began	a moose.
We saw	to snow.
My hat	hot chocolate.
The weather is	is spotty.
Jing drinks	really cold.

2. Can you write out one of the sentences you made in Question 1?

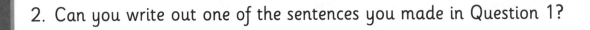

....

6

3. Tick the sentences that make sense.

The smiles polar bear seal at friendly the. ☐

Snow is Luba's favourite type of weather. ☐

We had sandwiches for our tea. ☐

The reindeer nose has red a. ☐

4. The words in the sentences below are in the wrong order.
Can you rewrite each sentence with the words in the right order?

The plays outside dog.

....

snowmen two builds Beth.

....

Claire the Bear has got her words mixed up and Bruce the Moose can't understand what she's saying. Can you work out what Claire's trying to say?

scarf a have I new .

my It hat matches .

like you it Do ?

How go it did? Oops!
How did it go?

 ☐ ☐ ☐

7

Using 'and'

The word **and** can be used to join two words together.

They ate fish and chips.

You can also use **and** to join sentences together.

Lola went shopping. She got some bread.

Lola went shopping and she got some bread.

1. Write the word **and** in the right box in each sentence.

We [ ] eat cheese [ ] grapes.

Tyson [ ] Colette drink [ ] juice.

I like [ ] broccoli [ ] carrots.

2. Can you join the sentences in the boxes together using **and**?
   Write the new sentence on the lines.

   He has a banana.   I have a pear.

   ....

   ....

3. Draw lines to join these sentences with **and**.

I like pizza

we all eat.

and

Dad cooks

and

George ices them.

and

Put the kettle on

you like burgers.

and

Rosa makes the cakes

make a cup of tea.

An Extra Challenge

Hasan wrote a recipe for his favourite sandwich, but he forgot to use **and**. Can you spot the places where the word **and** should go?

Take two slices of bread spread butter on them.

Add jam ketchup to one slice of bread.

Put the other slice of bread on top cut the sandwich in half.

Were these pages tasty and delicious? Put a tick in a box.

Capital letters and full stops

How It Works

Sentences always start with a capital letter
and they usually end with a full stop.

The pig played in the mud.

capital letter   full stop

Now Try These

1. Tick the sentences that use capital letters and full stops correctly.

the chickens play in the farmyard. ☐

You want to be a farmer. ☐

the cows mooed loudly at Kate ☐

We sat on the big red tractor. ☐

2. Write the word in the box with a capital letter
   and add a full stop to each sentence.

she ➡ .... really likes cows ☐

this ➡ .... farm has lots of animals ☐

he ➡ .... loves going to the farm ☐

3. Circle the letters that should be capital letters in the text below.

this is Brian the goat. he lives on a farm. the farmer also has chickens, two pigs and a cow. the farm is a nice place to live and Brian is very happy there. he always has a smile on his face.

4. Rewrite each sentence below using a capital letter and a full stop.

a sheep looked at me

....

the ducks ran away

....

An Extra Challenge

Samira is going to visit her friend Sheldon the Sheep, but she needs to cross his field without getting muddy. Can you help her reach Sheldon by making a path across the field? The right path uses capital letters and full stops correctly.

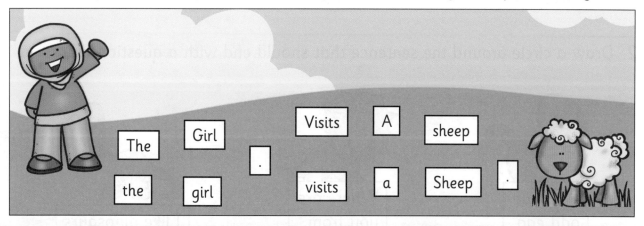

| The | Girl | | Visits | A | sheep | |
| the | girl | . | visits | a | Sheep | . |

Oink! How did you find these pages? Give a box a tick.

11

Question marks and exclamation marks

Questions always end with a question mark.

Where is the dinosaur?
question mark

What is your name?

Exclamation marks show strong feelings like anger or surprise. They can also show that someone is speaking loudly.

You scared me!
exclamation mark

Look at his teeth!

Now Try These

1. Finish each sentence by adding a question mark or an exclamation mark.

It's exploding ☐   Why are you blue ☐   Run away ☐

2. Draw a circle around the sentence that should end with a question mark.

What an odd egg   Where are you from   I like dinosaurs

3. Colour in a question mark or an exclamation mark to show how each sentence should end.

Did you see the T. rex

The egg has hatched

What's for dinner

4. Write each sentence next to the picture that it matches.

Who are you?   Don't fall off!

....

....

An Extra Challenge

What do you think the people in the picture are saying?

Make up one sentence that ends with a question mark and one sentence that ends with an exclamation mark.

Are you roar-some at question marks and exclamation marks?

Capital letters for names and 'I'

How It Works

The names of people and places start with a capital letter.

 Italy

Paris

Henry

The days of the week and the months of the year also start with a capital letter.

Monday   Friday   June   November

The word **I** should always be a capital letter.

 Jamil and i love flying.   Jamil and I love flying.

Now Try These

1. Colour in the pictures where the word should start with a capital letter.

 america

 trip

 charlie

 holiday

 paint

 i

 zebra

 london

 july

 smile

 saturday

2. Complete each word by adding the right capital letter.

(d) ....anielle   (e) ....gypt   (a) ....ugust   (t) ....uesday

3. Circle the words that should start with a capital letter in each sentence. In the box below, rewrite each word you circled using a capital letter.

In the summer, lucy is going to spain.

Last wednesday, i went on a steam train.

My sister fiona was born in january.

Take a look at this picture of an airport. Can you find all of the words that need a capital letter?

september

bags

bench

plane

james

desk

tilly

germany

sunday

Did you fly through these pages? Give a box a tick.

Spelling

How It Works

There are five vowels in the alphabet:

a e i o u

Vowels help make lots of different sounds. Here are two examples:

The **short oo** sound can be written **u** or **oo**.

bull   wood

The **ai** sound can be written **ai**, **ay** or **a_e**.

rain   clay   made

Now Try These

1. Colour in the pictures where the word is spelt correctly.

push

cook

gud

boosh

stood

buk

2. Complete each word with the right spelling of the **ai** sound.

Superheroes like to pl............... games.

She is going to catch the tr...............n.

Their outfits are not the s........m........ .

3. The **air** sound can be spelt **air**, **ear** or **are**. Circle the word in each sentence that has the right spelling of the **air** sound.

Is that a flying **bear** / **bair** ?

Ellen's **chare** / **chair** is really fast.

We always **shair** / **share** our sweets.

4. The **or** sound can be spelt **or**, **aw** or **au**. Can you rewrite each word below using the right spelling of the **or** sound?

sawce

....

dror

....

shaut

....

An Extra Challenge

Mr Whiskers the cat is stuck in a tree and everyone is talking about it. Can you correct their spelling mistakes to find out what's happening?

Help — I'm scaired of heights.

Don't worry Mr Whiskers. I'll sayve you!

It'll be OK! Just stai still and don't luk down!

I tried to help, but Mr Whiskers is afrade of hawses.

How super are you at spelling?
Tick a box to show how you did.

The princess and the dragon

Once upon a time, there was a princess called Evie. She and her family were always having unusual adventures. The book below tells the story of one of their adventures, but some of the pictures have fallen out.

Can you work out where the missing pictures should go? Draw a line from each picture on the right to show where it belongs in the story.

1

One day, Evie and her parents found something strange in their garden. It was a dragon!

2

The dragon kidnapped Evie's father, King Kyle, and locked him up in a deep, dark cave.

4

?

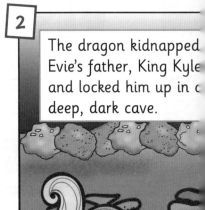

5

In a puff of smoke, the dragon turned into a small, fluffy dog. The cage fell apart, and King Kyle was free.

Evie set off through the woods to rescue her father. On the way, she found a wand lying on the ground.

When Evie reached the cave, she held the wand tightly and waved it at the dragon.

3

?

6

What do you think happened at the end of the story? Draw a picture of it in this box.

Tricky words

How It Works

Sometimes the same sound is written differently in different words.

When a word ends in the **tch** sound, it can be written:

ch

branch

tch

clutch

Now Try These

1. Draw lines to join the start of each word to the right ending.

ma____

ri____

i____

su____

ch

tch

lun____

fe____

swi____

ea____

2. The **w** sound can be written **w** or **wh**.
   Unscramble the letters in bold to make words with the **w** sound.

Don't fall in the **tewar**! ....

I don't know **eehrw** we are.  ....

Karim usually **kwlsa** to school. ➡  ....

20

3. The **f** sound can be written **f** or **ph**. Can you write these words in the box with the right spelling of the **f** sound?

ele___ant

roo___

care___ul

al___abet

lea___

4. Circle the right spelling of each word.

bench / bentch

wich / which

snach / snatch

phear / fear

wait / whait

An Extra Challenge

Jo wrote a diary entry about her class trip to the nature park, but she spelt some words wrong. How many mistakes can you spot? Can you correct them?

I had so mutch phun yesterday.

Whe played with leaves that had

phallen off the trees. I love hearing

the cruntch wen you jump in them.

My teacher took this foto of everyone.

Did you think these pages were a walk in the park? Tick a box.

Compound words

How It Works

A compound word is a word that is made up of two other words.

tooth brush  toothbrush

foot ➕ ball ▬ football

Now Try These

1. Can you fill in the missing letters in these compound words?
Use the picture clues to help you.

b................... b...................   c................... c...................

2. Circle the compound word in each sentence below.

His hairbrush is pink.

My cowboy hat is too big.

Her backpack is full of books.

Let's go to the playground.

I like your earrings.

3. Draw lines to join each pair of words that makes a compound word.
   Can you write the compound words in the box?

door   sun   pan

flower   cake   bell

4. Complete each sentence with a compound word made from the
   words in the boxes. Make sure the words are in the right order.

room   bed   Logan is in his ....

note   pad   Asha wrote on the ....

day   birth   It is Kai's ....

An Extra Challenge

Marley the Monkey and his friends are playing outside.
How many different compound words can you spot in Marley's garden?

Do you daydream about
compound words? Tick a box.

23

Rhymes

How It Works

Rhymes are words that have the same sound at the end.

sheep   keep   deep   leap

Saying words out loud can help you
to work out if they rhyme.

Now Try These

1. Draw lines to join the words that rhyme.

flower

dig

tree

bee

shower

big

2. Write out the word that rhymes with
   the underlined word in each sentence.

   They had so much <u>fun</u> when the sun came out.

   ....

   The rabbit <u>hopped</u> and then it stopped.

   ....

3. Colour in the things that rhyme with **spring**.

sing

slide

snail

swing

4. Circle the words in each column that rhyme with the word at the top.

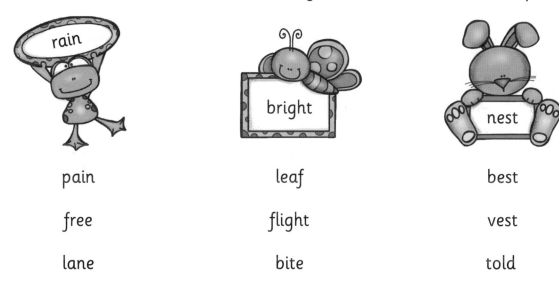

rain

bright

nest

pain	leaf	best
free	flight	vest
lane	bite	told

An Extra Challenge

Olga and her friends are having fun in the spring sunshine. How many different words can you think of that rhyme with each word in the picture?

blow

splash

fly

ride

How did these pages go? Tick a box to show what you know.

Odd one out

How It Works

Pieces of writing sometimes have pictures with them. Sometimes, the pictures might not match the words.

The cake is decorated with jam and icing.

The bear doesn't belong in the cake.

Some sentences might not fit in with the rest of the writing.

This is my grandma's recipe. It makes twenty biscuits.
Glasgow is in Scotland.

These sentences are about a biscuit recipe.

This sentence doesn't match the topic.

Now Try These

1. For each passage below, draw a circle around the picture that does not match the words.

The children were getting ready to bake. They found a cake tin and a mixing bowl on the shelf.

Next, they looked for all of the ingredients. They took eggs, butter and milk out of the fridge.

After several hours of hard work, the chocolate cake and the apple pie were finally ready to eat.

2. Circle the two sentences that do not match the picture.

Sami is going to the park.

The children are baking.

Isaac is covered in sticky icing.

There is a pie in the kitchen.

You find shells on the beach.

Eliza is mixing the ingredients.

3. Tick the sentences below that match the topic.

Brilliant Baking

Flour is used to make cakes and bread.

Chocolate and lemon are both popular cake flavours.

Hedgehogs usually sleep during the winter.

An Extra Challenge

Mina, Thandi and Kevin are describing what they did yesterday. Can you spot who is the odd one out? What makes them different from the others?

I played tennis with my dad.

I went to the bakery to buy some bread.

Mina

Thandi

I went to work at the bakery.

Kevin

Bakery

How did you get on? Were these pages a piece of cake?

27

More than one sentence

How It Works

You can join lots of sentences together to make a story. The sentences need to be in the right order so that the story makes sense.

Ava got dressed. Then she woke up.

The events are in the wrong order, so this doesn't make sense.

Ava woke up. Then she got dressed.

This does make sense. The events are in the right order.

Now Try These

1. Use the pictures to put the sentences below in the right order, using the numbers 1 to 5. The first one has been done for you.

Ava was upset — she thought everyone had forgotten her birthday. ☐

Outside, there was a surprise party with all of her friends. ☐

It was Ava's birthday and she couldn't wait to celebrate. 1

Ava's cousins jumped out, holding balloons and cheering. ☐

When she got downstairs, there were no balloons or presents. ☐

2. These pictures show what happens next, but they're in the wrong order.
   Can you write a sentence to describe what is happening in each picture?
   Then put the pictures in the right order, using the numbers 1 to 3.

....

....

....

....

....

....

....

....

An Extra Challenge

The pictures below show Ava's friend Leo getting ready for her party,
but they're in the wrong order. Can you put them in the right order?

He carefully wrapped
it in blue paper.

Finally, he put a
big bow on the top.

Leo bought a present
for Ava's birthday.

Is putting sentences in order
your party trick? Tick a box.

What happens next?

You can guess what happens next in a text by reading it carefully to find clues.

This tells you what Polly wants to do.

Polly the Pirate decided to buy a pet parrot. She saw a pet shop across the road.

This gives her a way of getting a parrot.

What do you think Polly did next?

She got a parrot. ✓   She went home. ☐   She got a dog. ☐

Now Try These

It was Obasi's first day at pirate school. Lesson one was how to clean the ship. He picked up his bucket and mop.

1. What do you think Obasi did next? Tick one box.

He cleaned the ship. ☐   He played with his friends. ☐

He went swimming. ☐   He did his homework. ☐

After the lesson, Obasi and his friends were hungry. They went to the kitchen and spotted some biscuits.

2. What do you think they did next? Circle one answer.

They left the kitchen.

They ate the biscuits.

They cooked lunch.

The next lesson was swimming. Polly was the fastest swimmer at pirate school. She had a swimming race with Obasi.

3. What do you think happened next? Colour the hat above the right answer.

Obasi won the race.

Polly won the race.

They fed Polly's parrot.

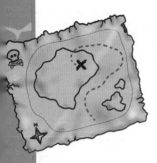

The last lesson was steering the ship. The teacher told them what to do and pointed at an island on the map. Ola took hold of the ship's wheel and began to steer.

4. What do you think happened next?

....

....

An Extra Challenge

Looking at pictures can also help you work out what happens next.
Look carefully at the pictures below. What do you think will happen next?

How did it go? Did you work out what happened next?

Writing to people

How It Works

You can write to people to stay in touch with them.

You might write to someone to:

⭐ say thank you

⭐ let them know how you are

⭐ invite them somewhere

Now Try These

Dear Aunt Fatima,

It's my birthday on Saturday and I'm going to be six! I'm really excited because I'm going to go to the funfair with all my friends.

Love from Owen

Mrs F. Larker
16 Early Rise
Middle Dollop
DO6 7RX

1. When is Owen's birthday?

Monday ☐   Friday ☐   Saturday ☐

2. Circle the picture that shows how Owen feels about his birthday.

excited   sad   angry

3. Where is Owen going to go on his birthday?

....

4. Imagine you're having a birthday party at the funfair. Fill in the gaps in the invitation below.

Write your address here.

....

....

....

....

Dear .... ,

Write your friend's name here.

Would you like to come to my birthday party at the funfair on Saturday?

I think you will have fun because ....

.... After the funfair we will go back to my

house to eat ....

I really hope you can come!

Write your name here.

Love from ....

An Extra Challenge

Oh dear! Owen wrote a thank you letter to Karen, but his dog has ripped it up.
Can you help Owen stick his letter back together in the right order?
You can use the invitation above to help you.

Thank you very much for giving me a toy for my birthday. I had a great time at the fair with you.

Love from Owen

23 Oak Street
New Town
Somershire
WA7 9JQ

Dear Karen,

See you soon!

Did you whizz through these pages? Give a box a tick.

33

Finding facts

How It Works

Some pieces of writing are full of facts. You can find facts by reading the text carefully and looking at the pictures.

This sentence tells you lots of facts:

Nefertiti **was** a queen in Ancient Egypt.

her name ↑   who she was ↗   where she lived ↗

Now Try These

Cleopatra

The Ancient Egyptians

The Ancient Egyptians lived by the River Nile thousands of years ago.

They were ruled by kings and queens, like Cleopatra.

When they died, some kings and queens were buried in giant pyramids in the desert.

Cats were very important to the Ancient Egyptians — people even prayed to them.

pyramids

1. Tick the sentences that are true.

     The Ancient Egyptians lived a hundred years ago. ☐

     Cleopatra was an Ancient Egyptian queen. ☐

     Some Ancient Egyptians were buried in pyramids. ☐

     Cats were not important to the Ancient Egyptians. ☐

2. Which river did the Ancient Egyptians live next to?

....

Read these texts carefully. Use them to answer the questions below.

ANUBIS

Anubis was the Ancient Egyptian god of the dead.

Anubis had the head of a dog.

ISIS

Isis was the Ancient Egyptian goddess of magic.

She had strong healing powers.

3. Anubis had the head of which animal? Circle one answer.

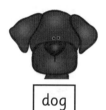

dog

crocodile

cat

lion

4. What was Isis the goddess of? Circle one answer.

the sun

rainbows

magic

the dead

An Extra Challenge

Read the fact file that Seth the Ancient Egyptian made about himself.

Can you make a fact file about yourself? Make sure you include:

- your name
- how old you are
- where you live
- what your favourite hobby is

SETH

I am five years old.

I live in Ancient Egypt.

My favourite hobby is riding camels.

How did you find that? Are you an expert on Ancient Egypt?

Answers

Pages 2-3 — Nouns

1. spade, bucket, shell, shorts
2. You should have circled: book, lemon, horse, shoe, car
3. He went on the <u>slide</u>.
   I have a purple <u>coat</u>.
   Your <u>cat</u> is hungry.
   She made a tasty <u>cake</u>.
   The <u>water</u> was very cold.
4. I played in the <u>sand</u>.
   My sister has a pet <u>hamster</u>.

   An Extra Challenge

   Any sensible nouns, e.g. ball, girls, boy, lolly, sandals, sun, pool, shorts

Pages 4-5 — Verbs

1. You should have coloured: hop, walk, sing, shout
2. You should have circled: I have brown hair.
   We read our books.
   You bake a cake.
3. Noah <u>swims</u> really fast.
   They <u>ride</u> their bikes.
   I <u>do</u> the splits.

   An Extra Challenge

   Koji skips. / Tom and Mia stretch. / Orli runs.
   I skip. / I stretch. / I run.

Pages 6-7 — Making sentences

1. We saw a moose.
   My hat is spotty.
   The weather is really cold.
   Jing drinks hot chocolate.
2. Any sentence from Question 1.
3. You should have ticked: Snow is Luba's favourite type of weather.
   We had sandwiches for our tea.
4. The dog plays outside.
   Beth builds two snowmen.

   An Extra Challenge

   I have a new scarf. It matches my hat. Do you like it?

Pages 8-9 — Using 'and'

1. We eat cheese <u>and</u> grapes.
   Tyson <u>and</u> Colette drink juice.
   I like broccoli <u>and</u> carrots.
2. He has a banana and I have a pear.
   OR I have a pear and he has a banana.
3. Dad cooks and we all eat.
   Put the kettle on and make a cup of tea.
   Rosa makes the cakes and George ices them.

   An Extra Challenge

   Take two slices of bread <u>and</u> spread butter on them.

   Add jam <u>and</u> ketchup to one slice of bread.

   Put the other slice of bread on top <u>and</u> cut the sandwich in half.

Pages 10-11 — Capital letters and full stops

1. You should have ticked: You want to be a farmer.
   We sat on the big red tractor.
2. She really likes cows.
   This farm has lots of animals.
   He loves going to the farm.
3. <u>t</u>his is Brian the goat. <u>h</u>e lives on a farm. <u>t</u>he farmer also has chickens, two pigs and a cow. <u>t</u>he farm is a nice place to live and Brian is very happy there. <u>h</u>e always has a smile on his face.
4. A sheep looked at me.
   The ducks ran away.

   An Extra Challenge

   You should have made this sentence: The girl visits a sheep.

Pages 12-13 — Question marks and exclamation marks

1. It's exploding!
   Why are you blue?
   Run away!
2. You should have circled: Where are you from?
3. Did you see the T. rex?
   The egg has hatched!
   What's for dinner?
4. Don't fall off!
   Who are you?

Answers

An Extra Challenge

Any sensible sentences that end with the right punctuation mark, e.g. We found three dinosaurs! Where did they come from?

Pages 14-15 — Capital letters for names and 'I'

1. You should have coloured: america, charlie, i, london, july, saturday

2. Danielle, Egypt, August, Tuesday

3. In the summer, <u>lucy</u> is going to <u>spain</u>.
   Last <u>wednesday</u>, <u>i</u> went on a steam train.
   My sister <u>fiona</u> was born in <u>january</u>.
   Lucy, Spain, Wednesday, I, Fiona, January

   An Extra Challenge

   september, james, tilly, germany, sunday

Pages 16-17 — Spelling

1. You should have coloured: push, cook, stood

2. Superheroes like to <u>play</u> games.
   She is going to catch the <u>train</u>.
   Their outfits are not the <u>same</u>.

3. Is that a flying <u>bear</u>?
   Ellen's <u>chair</u> is really fast.
   We always <u>share</u> our sweets.

4. sauce, draw, short

   An Extra Challenge

   Help — I'm <u>scared</u> of heights.

   Don't worry Mr Whiskers. I'll <u>save</u> you!

   I tried to help, but Mr Whiskers is <u>afraid</u> of <u>horses</u>.

   It'll be OK! Just <u>stay</u> still and don't <u>look</u> down.

Pages 18-19 — The princess and the dragon

Evie set off through the woods... — 3

When Evie reached the cave... — 4

Any drawing that completes the story in a sensible way.

Pages 20-21 — Tricky words

1. match, rich, itch, such, lunch, fetch, switch, each
2. water, where, walks
3. elephant, roof, careful, alphabet, leaf
4. You should have circled: bench, which, snatch, fear, wait

An Extra Challenge

I had so <u>much</u> <u>fun</u> yesterday. <u>We</u> played with leaves that had <u>fallen</u> off the trees. I love hearing the <u>crunch</u> <u>when</u> you jump in them. My teacher took this <u>photo</u> of everyone.

Pages 22-23 — Compound words

1. birdbath, cupcake

2. My <u>cowboy</u> hat is too big.
   His <u>hairbrush</u> is pink.
   Her <u>backpack</u> is full of books.
   Let's go to the <u>playground</u>.
   I like your <u>earrings</u>.

3. doorbell, sunflower, pancake

4. Logan is in his <u>bedroom</u>.
   Asha wrote on the <u>notepad</u>.
   It is Kai's <u>birthday</u>.

   An Extra Challenge

   Any compound words that appear in the picture, e.g. armchair, popcorn, rainbow, watermelon, skateboard, sunglasses, teacup, teapot, tablecloth, basketball, sunshine

Pages 24-25 — Rhymes

1. flower — shower
   dig — big
   tree — bee

2. sun, stopped

3. You should have coloured: sing, swing

4. rain — pain, lane
   bright — flight, bite
   nest — best, vest

   An Extra Challenge

   Any words that rhyme with the words in the picture, e.g.
   blow — slow, grow, flow, know, toe
   splash — flash, crash, smash, trash, dash
   fly — high, try, spy, lie, eye
   ride — hide, side, tried, cried, bride

Pages 26-27 — Odd one out

1. You should have circled the bag of sugar, the jar of marmalade and the doughnut.

2. You should have circled: Sami is going to the park.
   You find shells on the beach.

Answers

3. You should have ticked: Flour is used to make cakes and bread.
Chocolate and lemon are both popular cake flavours.

An Extra Challenge

Thandi is the odd one out because she played tennis, but everyone else went to the bakery.

Pages 28-29 — More than one sentence

1. Ava was upset — she thought everyone had forgotten her birthday. — 3
Outside, there was a surprise party with all of her friends. — 5
It was Ava's birthday and she couldn't wait to celebrate. — 1
Ava's cousins jumped out, holding balloons and cheering. — 4
When she got downstairs, there were no balloons or presents. — 2

2. Any sensible sentences that describe the pictures, e.g.
Everyone had sausages and burgers for tea. — 2
Mum told Ava it was time for bed. — 3
The children played games in the garden. — 1

An Extra Challenge

He carefully wrapped it in blue paper. — 2
Finally, he put a big bow on the top. — 3
Leo bought a present for Ava's birthday. — 1

Pages 30-31 — What happens next?

1. You should have ticked: He cleaned the ship.
2. You should have circled: They ate the biscuits.
3. You should have coloured: Polly won the race.
4. Any sensible answer, e.g. Ola steered the ship to the island.

An Extra Challenge

Any sensible suggestion, e.g. The boy will dig up some treasure.

Pages 32-33 — Writing to people

1. You should have ticked: Saturday
2. You should have circled: excited
3. the funfair
4. Any sensible answers.

An Extra Challenge

23 Oak Street
New Town
Somershire
WA7 9JQ

Dear Karen,
Thank you very much for giving me a toy for my birthday. I had a great time at the fair with you.
See you soon!
Love from Owen

Pages 34-35 — Finding facts

1. You should have ticked:
Cleopatra was an Ancient Egyptian queen.
Some Ancient Egyptians were buried in pyramids.
2. the River Nile
3. You should have circled: dog
4. You should have circled: magic

An Extra Challenge

Any sensible answers.